To Susan
— with much love —

Jack   12-10-2013

Jack Grapes, "Self-Portrait," 2008
oil on canvas, 18 x 24

POEMS
SO FAR

SO FAR
SO GOOD

SO FAR
TO GO

JACK GRAPES

Bombshelter Press
Los Angeles, CA 2014

ACKNOWLEDGEMENTS

Some of the poems in this collection originally appeared in *The Cultural Weekly* and as broadsides from 48th Street Press,
Caracas Venezuela.

ISBN: 978-1493607754

BOMBSHELTER PRESS
www.bombshelterpress.com
books@bombshelterpress.com
PO Box 481266 Bicentennial Station
Los Angeles, California 90048 USA

Printed in the United States of America

To
Josh
&
Daniele

"It is because I used to think of certain things, of certain people, that the things, the people, and these alone, I still take seriously, still give me joy. Whether it be that the faith which creates has ceased to exist in me, or that reality will take shape in the memory alone, there has awakened in me that anguish which, later on in life, transfers itself to the passion of love, and may even become its inseperable companion."

–Marcel Proust

CONTENTS

"The reader, the thinker, the loiterer, the *flâneur*, are types of illuminati just as much as the opium eater, the dreamer, the ecstatic. And more profane. Not to mention that most terrible drug — ourselves — which we take in solitude."

−Walter Benjamin
Art in the Age of Mechanical Reproduction

LOST LAKE

What happens when you try
believing in God is things begin
to fall apart.
Like when we were lost
trying to find Lost Lake
high in the high
Sierras, leaning against
a large boulder unable
to go on, munching
gorp from our army pack
and ready to fall
in the snow and call it
quits. I remember that
to this day. Calling it
quits, I mean. My old
football coach Mr. Palone
would have killed me
if he'd known I was ready
to call it quits,
and the irony, Lost Lake
was only 30 yards away,
over the next rise,
gleaming and teeming
with fish.
That's what happens when
you climb miles
with a fifty pound backback
in the high Sierras,
and the beauty of nature
makes you believe in God
and then things begin to fall apart.
I suppose it's somewhat like love.
You believe in love and then
things begin to fall apart.
Better not to believe in it,

but what happens when it comes
to you, brown-eyed and wishing
only the best for you?
Can love be returned even
when you don't believe in it?
A part of me is still leaning
against that boulder,
next to my best friend Allan,
who in his own way,
had given up too,
and I've never known Allan
to ever give up on anything.
But we both had had it.
So we leaned against that stone
and ate our gorp, biding our time,
assuming that what is lost
is never lost forever,
and like love, comes looking for you
when you least expect it,
even when you've stopped
believing in it.

SEATED NUDE

Went to dinner tonight at Muddy Leak, then to see *The Heart of Darkness* at the Actor's Gang. I found myself staring off into the distance, tuning out the play, thinking of Modigliani's painting the "Seated Nude," painted in 1916 while he worked mostly on portraits, not a period when he was concentrating on the female form. Modigliani was also a sculptor, and of the twenty-four or so surviving sculptures that he made after a decisive meeting with Brancusi in 1909, only two are nudes. Yet, it was the female form that preoccupied him, judging by the drawings he left behind. There is something ancient and primitive in that painting, with the model shown head on, her figure filling the canvas, her body diagonal against the blue background and the slanting rail on the left, giving it a sense of disequilibrium. The model's body is thrust forward, uninhibited by her nakedness, while the inclination of her head, her blushing face and closed eyes reveal a vulnerability or reserve, perhaps even a knowing languor. Find one of Titian's nudes, and you will be reminded of this painting, those brush strokes comparable to the chisel-marks in some of Modigliani's sculptures. I think I first encountered those long-necked women of Modigliani's when I was in college, and they have haunted me ever since, so to see "Seated Nude" today at LACMA was a special treat. I'm not even sure why the image has haunted me today. Even amidst the rantings of Mr. Kurtz in *the Heart of Darkness*, my mind drifted to the langour of that nude. During chit-chatty dinner conversation over smoked salmon and poached eggs, I'd tilt my head down or gaze off into the distance, drifting off into a kind of sadness, as if the painting itself were attached to some great wound within me. Such loveliness persists despite the encroachments of the moment. I wanted to be back in the museum, standing before the painting, gathering in those brushstrokes and flat planes of light, the model's wispy pubic hairs and painterly skin. Like the siren song, Modigliani called to me, and I followed that voice to the rocks where oblivion stronger than any drug, except the drug of love resides. Then bill came and I left a hefty tip, all the while thinking of Modigliani's "Seated Nude," longing and sadness entwined within. I looked at my watch, checked back into the world, the world that Wordsworth says is too much with us, we who get and spend and lay waste our powers. I was still longing for that other world, that motionless and timeless world of art, the Great Art that sustains me as I travel this last, downward sloping phase of my life.

A SMALL CABIN IN THE WOODS

You're old enough to get in your car and drive out to some forest on the edge of town. What you take with you tells us a lot about you. Perhaps a tablet to write on, perhaps a roll of scotch tape, perhaps a bag of cough drops. In the middle of the forest is a small pond, the water so cold you couldn't breathe that time you fell into it. And later, the forest ranger came by and asked what you did to the rattlesnake you killed with a large rock there were so many holes in his skin. If you look around, you can find the things you need to build a small cabin. Small, but large enough for your roll of scotch tape and the cough drops. The tablet you might have to leave outside. And you probably forgot to bring a pencil or a pen, so the tablet is useless anyway. You can sleep standing up. What nestles in your heart is love. It's odorless and colorless. But at night, when you're sleeping, you can hear it walking around, from chamber to chamber, trying to say something. If you knew what it was saying, you might be able to follow its instructions. Head for the hills, it might be saying, or maybe just something simple, like, you big dope, why didn't you bring a pencil or a pen. Love can be a bitter pill. When it's dark, it likes to crack jokes. Or quote lines from Greek poetry. You're old enough to know better, to tell the heart to go to sleep, to tell the heart to shut up. But all night long it mumbles, trying to wake you from a sleep you've slept all your life. One time, in the supermarket, the heart called out to you as you were selecting a cabbage for soup. Wake up, it said. I am fucking awake, you replied. No you're not, said love, walking around inside your heart, from chamber to chamber. I'm too old to wake up, you said, as you put the cabbage back. No you're not, the voice of love inside your heart said. Now, you're sleeping, standing in the cabin you built in the middle of some forest on the edge of town. A small cabin. Small, but large enough to stand in. A voice telling you to wake up. You're not too old to wake up.

THE MOON & SIXPENCE

Since the email I got a few days ago about the moon,
I got to thinking about Shakespeare,
as I often do,
usually when I'm getting gas for my car,
or brushing my teeth
(another way of saying I'm always thinking of Shakespeare),
and thought of all the appearances of the moon
the Bard offered in the way of his two cents.

Last night, I had one of those nice evenings at home,
reading, working on my book, shuffling around in my study.
I went out to find the moon but she hadn't risen yet,
but later, when I went out back to check on the Laker's collapse,
there she was, up in a tree, sliding back and forth
whichever way I went, as if trying to hide,
or make me come after her.

Then I remembered Othello:

"It is the very error of the moon;
She comes more nearer earth than she was wont,
And makes men mad."

But even Fair Juliet knew there was something about the moon
to be suspicious of.
When Romeo tells her that he will
swear by "yonder blessed moon that tips with silver all these fruit-tree tops,"
she puts her hand to his mouth and shuts it:

"O, swear not by the moon, the inconstant moon,
That monthly changes in her circled orb,
Lest that thy love prove likewise variable."

And poor klutzy teenage Romeo frowns and scratches his head.

"What shall I swear by?" he asks,
like a bad algebra student
unable to figure the value of x.
   "Do not swear at all," says Juliet,
"Or, if thou wilt, swear by thy gracious self,
Which is the god of my idolatry,
And I'll believe thee."

One needn't be Shakespeare to know the moon's conjugations.
As Titania says in *Midsummer Night's Dream*,
"Therefore, the moon, that governess of floods,
Pale in her anger, washes all the air."

Shakespeare calls it an envious moon,
a fleeting moon,
a perilous moon,
a moon that looks bloody
on the earth.

I marveled last night as I stood looking up at it
through the backyard trees.
I decided not to be infected
by Newton's mind and the laws of gravity,
but to see the moon
as Shakespeare saw it,
and let it have power over me,
and I knew why it was that we are made
mad to write poetry:
perilous poetry,
envious poetry,
bloody poetry.

Then, we wake, and return to the pedestrian earth,
the earth of bank deposits,
post-offices trips,
supermarket catch-ups,
copy machines and office supplies,
and all the other mundane tasks we perform under the sun.

The sun that exposes things as they are,
not what they can be

under the bloody moon.

BOB'S POETRY

Bob writes poetry
as if poetry
were going out of style.
Everything is fading: the darkness,
the morning mist, the light
in the piazza, the life his sister
guarded with her teeth.
Some things wane; regrets
exist only late in the night
when others are sleeping;
the self is either unknown
or unguarded; sonatas are sweet;
chances squandered, lives lived
fully.
In the corner by lamplight
Dad or Mom grows older,
sharpening futile promises,
leaving a trail of sparks.
Like the Dude, Death
abides.
Waits its turn.
Doesn't stand on ceremony.
Doesn't hold its breath.
Doesn't make deals.

I like Bob's poetry.
It doesn't pull any punches.
Poetry may, in fact, be going out of style.
If not for Bob, we could all be reading
journalism, or worse, roadmaps.
If not for Bob, who writes poetry
as if poetry
were going out of style,
we'd all forget to sing
in the car

on the way
to the airport
bound for a country
no one
in his right mind
would visit.

LAKE PONTCHARTRAIN SEAWALL

Not too many stones here
on the cement wall by the lake,
nor on the cement steps
that descend into the black water,
six deep at high tide, two deep at low.
We used to put a stone on the steps
for every girl we necked with
in the back seat of our '56 Chevies
parked a few feet from the shoreline wall.
One summer, there must have been
a hundred stones along the concrete top.
The hurricanes would come in late August,
early September.
By fall, there was not one stone left;
all had been carried off into the lake.
Just seawall and concrete,
far as the eye could see, from Lakeview
to the Pontchartrain Causeway.
Sometimes, in January or February,
a stone would appear here, another over there.
But they didn't last long.
High winter waves from Gulf storms
would wash them back into the lake.
One summer, Peter Bordelon decided
that if you broke up with a girl,
you'd walk down to the seawall,
pick up a stone, and skip it onto the waters
of the lake, the dark placid waters
that greedily swallowed
that offering to the god of teenage love,
so you'd always remember
that it was you who reached down
and threw the stone away,
not the fickle red-head
buttoning her blouse in the front seat

of your car, anxious to get home
to her bucket of stones.

LIFE IS A MOTORBIKE

But love is a translucent motorbike.
As the poets say,
we see through a glass darkly.
Light is able to pass through,
but so diffused
that objects
are not clearly visible.
This is how it is with love.
We know it is there,
but we do not always see it clearly.
So some of us make things,
some of us paint pictures,
some of us put words
out into
the universe
and try to connect the dots
so love appears clearer, is
shaped into an object we can imagine,
if not truly see.
If your life doesn't begin with love,
perhaps it will end with love.
And if love
doesn't reduce you to tears,
if it doesn't make crazy with sporadic logic,
something is amiss,
either with you,
or with love.

What we can do
is build a fire inside a circle of stones
and do our dance together.
Around that fire.
This summer began with a supermoon,
and will end with our words,
words that,

like love,
will reduce us to tears,
and make our minds
crazy with sporadic logic.
Because I always begin with love.
And if I am lucky,
I will end with love as well.

UNEXPECTEDLY

I'm always finding things that I don't remember losing.
A set of keys, a book, a phone number, even this poem,
which I unexpectedly found tucked inside a book I'd also lost,
along with a phone number.
I couldn't remember whose number it was,
and was hesitant to call it,
for fear it might be someone I don't want
to talk to. For days I thought about that series of numbers
which reconfigured in my head as I drove
around the city, running errands, meeting a client,
buying paper and paper clips. At some point,
the numbers reassembled and I couldn't remember
the exact order anymore.
Was it 504-822-3006, or 822-306-0504,
or maybe 405-282-6003?
I lost interest in who belonged to the numbers,
it was the numbers themselves that attached
to my brain. Sometimes, when talking,
the numbers would just spill out of my mouth,
unexpectedly, like "I'm looking for 60 pound $8^{1/2}$ by 11
recycled paper 405-603-0282, 90 brightness."
Or when making love, I might say
"Oooh, I love you so 360-054-8022."
I remember standing in an open field and watching
dawn come up, also unexpectedly,
because I had been mired so deeply in the night,
broken heart and lost resolve,
that I had lost faith in even the dependable sun
from ever reclaiming the sky.
I wanted night to last so long, I'd never see
the sun again, never see a blue sky,
never be reminded of how sweet life was,
how fillled it was with the tiniest moments
of pleasure.
How I ended up in the middle of that field

I'm not sure. One minute I was staring out the window
of my apartment, across the alley, at a brick wall,
and the next I'm in the middle of an open field.
I had just separated from my wife,
and there was a bottle of elevil my therapist
had given me to relieve my depression,
and the thought occured to me that I could
just take the whole bottle and be done with it,
but then I'd have to go through my journals --
there were 63 of them at the time,
in fire-proof boxes at the bottom of the closet --
and cut out the parts I didn't want people to read.
I held the bottle of pills in my hand and walked to the window,
looked out at the brick wall,
a brick wall that seemed to be the perfect
metaphor at that time for my life,
and next thing I knew I was standing in that field,
watching dawn   rosy-fingered dawn
come up, unexpectedly.
For a moment, I thought I was in another poem,
"Walking the Wilderness" by William Stafford,
or maybe that poem by Mark Strand,
"Absence of Field."
How nice, I thought, to end up in a poem.

PERFECT

Before when it was imperfect
it was perfect like how I love you
and how you love me and how
imperfectly we kiss or hold each
other in some echo of
retention near dark where bodies
surrender their belongings
on the road
we traveled imperfectly
toward each other
closer year by year,
day by day,
minute by perfect minute
then we're here together
moving from the perfection
of gathering to the imperfection
of rocks green glass
stones on a bookshelf
marking the moons
in sync walking barefoot
in Paris stopping
to breathe the breath
of longing,
a field covered with snow
we called home.

GRAVITY

Everything is simple until it's hard
and then it seems it was never simple.

An orange falls to the ground
and the man looks at his watch
and imagines it's Tuesday.

One night I was older, and the next
day I was older still, but today,
as I write this, I am suddenly
young again, falling in love

with everything, including this
tomato that looks like a heart,
which makes it difficult for me
to cut it with a knife
but I do, slice right through it
you just slice right through it
and all the juice comes out and
I put it in my mouth
and it's good.

Tonight I saw the moon slide
behind a cloud, and oh, you should
have seen it, bright full moon
and I wondered, who is masquerading
as the moon, or is the moon
masquerading as someone else?
She moves behind another cloud,
hiding from me, and I sigh
and accept my loss.

My father died when he was fifty-four
and I'm seventy-one, well, I will be
seventy-one come September 11,

and my father had he lived to be seventy-one
would have died when I was thirty-seven.
My son still had yet to be born.
Not for another twelve years.
We named him after my father.
Now Josh is twenty-two, living on his own,
not far away from this house,
the house he grew up in.

Whether it's an apple or an orange,
all things eventually fall back to earth.
The moon will have its day too
to fall into the earth.
And if I'm still here,
I will open my arms to receive her,
even though both of us will be destroyed
in the end.
This moon belongs to me,
and I belong to the moon.
We are one conversation
circling each other in the mystery
of creation, reflecting the light
of the larger sun, that light
that draws us both toward
the center, toward
all that
fire.

A SOLITARY ROAD

A solitary road.
Someone singing a song.
Enormous in the sunshine.
The breath of darkness.
How much love have we known,
asks the Buddha sitting
by the side of the road.
Is that a rhetorical question,
I ask, or a question meant
for me to answer?
Buddha shrugs.
Who knows, he says, it's just
a question.
First you'd have to define the word *love*,
he says,
then the word *known*,
then, the hard part, you'd have to quantify
what is meant by the phrase *how much*.
The question's too complicated, he says,
and not worth answering.
But, he adds, it's a good question, dontcha think?
And I think, this Buddha's not much fun,
so I walk on.
It's a solitary road.
A different song now being sung,
but the same road, enormous
in the sunshine, the breath of darkness
leaning against the low hills in the distance.
I remember how I once
boiled an egg and ate it.
There was the time I held someone's hand
across a table, the feel of the tablecloth
under my outstretched arm.
One night, when I was five,
I saw my father,

chin resting on his fist,
somewhat like Rodin's "Thinker,"
and I tried to imagine what he was thinking,
my father, as lightning flashed and thunder
shook the house.
All solitary roads, enormous in the sunshine,
the breath of darkness raining
across the low hills in the distance.
An empty house by the side of the road.
I go in, call out a name, but she doesn't answer.
That's gone too. It was a name I whispered once,
when I was happy.
Now, not even an echo.
In the kitchen, a tuna sandwich, half-eaten,
sitting on a paper plate.
The only evidence she was here:
A half-eaten tuna sandwich
on a paper plate.
This makes me laugh for a time,
reminds me to laugh till my sides hurt,
to laugh along with others laughing,
so hard, everyone falls to the floor
exhausted. You're killing me,
they'd say, killing me.
A solitary road.
A song.
The breath of darkness.
Low hills in the distance.
The Buddha
asking questions
not meant
to be answered.

WHAT TO KEEP, WHAT TO GIVE AWAY

What I will take with me are the words.
You can have the rest,
the cars, the curtains, the silver spoons,
the chairs we sat in, the doors we
slammed, the windows we dressed,
the running shoes, the bow ties,
the suits, the hats, the glasses
we drank from, the cups
we smashed at the Greek restaurant
on Robertson.
I lingered a long time over passion,
then gave it up with the rest.
What is passion, after all,
but a longing for God.

"What'll you have?" asks the bartender.
"Passion," I say.
"I thought you gave that up with all the rest,"
he says.
"Yeah, I know, but it was a mistake,"
I say, "I've decided to take passion back."
"Then you're still longing for God,"
he says.

I should go to Barcelona.
Maybe Paris.
Rome would be nice.
St. Petersburg I hear is worth a trip.
You can get good dope in Copenhagen.
But what about Verona, or Miami?
Who in his right mind would want
to go to Miami?
Verona I can understand.
But Miami?

Listen, let me let you in on a little secret.
When I get there, my love will be waiting for me.
She'll have one of those flotation devices,
and tell me the water's fine,
I should just dive in.
She'll show me around the condominiun.
A desk where I can write, a shelf
for my favorite books,
and lots of sugarless chocolate bars
on the table I can eat to my heart's content.
And she's wearing a bathing suit to boot.
When was the last time I saw her
in a bathing suit? Can't remember.
But she's got great thighs.
She's wearing that bathing suit
and I can admire her thighs.
There she is, rising like Aphrodite
from the sea.
She was looking for me from the start,
found me running in circles,
came and got me, taught me
how to run in a straight line,
toward God.

Back to earth.
Millions of us.
In the oppressive heat.
A drink in the morning.
Connection to spherical power
and the ability to move
heavy objects.
Persistence with charm.
A star in the Southern sky.
You don't know where you're going.
A hawk circles overhead.
The calligraphy of bad manners.
A wicker basket filled
with all your mistakes.

A white bird in a golden cage.
Dreams that taste like strawberry popsicles.

Last night I heard her voice,
talking on the phone in the kitchen.
Her voice, along with the words,
and passion, that's what I'll take with me.

You can keep all the rest.

TWO-PART HARMONY

Accept that you carry death with you
in your pocket like a stone
you rub with thumb and forefinger
when life renders you invisible.
You can breath life back into those
who walk as if love
has been lost, as if they have choked
on their despair.
Today, I thought of all the ways I had buried
love and other figments of my imagination.
Need creeps upon you like a thief in the night.
Sometimes I think of you but I can't remember
exactly who you are. I must have loved you once
a long time ago, but all I remember
is a summer dress and the way it flapped
around you when you walked.
Two-part harmony is not hard
when you put your mind to it and try not to listen
to what the other person is singing.
She was a slow and dreamy dancer,
danced with me most of the night,
but went home with the other guy,
the one with the convertible
and the blue suede shoes.
You'd think if I lived this much
in my mind that I'd put up curtains,
but then you wouldn't be able to see in,
especially at night when the lights are on
and I'm lit up like a Christmas tree.
She tries to find the right word,
those of us who cherish solitude,
a hem and a haw and a stuttering vowel.
In Claude Lorraine's landscape
she'd be sitting under a tree,
the Great God Pan playing the flute

while revelers dance around her
drinking goblets of wine.
I'm not sure whether we're supposed
to find ourselves in love,
or lose ourselves in love.
Art is supposed to come to the rescue,
but some days, it doesn't,
some days you're left with empty hands,
some days you wish you didn't need art
to come to the rescue,
some days you wish you didn't need
to be rescued.
Thing is, when you're in need of rescue,
someone usually comes and finds you,
or maybe I'm just lucky that way.
What keeps me here is love, plain and simple.
I can't for the life of me figure it out.
It's the world, buckeroos, that breaks the heart,
not the loved one. The world
will always break your heart,
that's the deal.
If you can find that place
where you are broken,
and give thanks that you allowed it,
you jumped in, both feet,
you took the deal
and now you're aching with it,
the loss and the yearning
and the gratitude and the dread.
If you can do that,
you will find everything you need
to carry on one more day,
one more day
on this earth
while death waits
in your pocket
like a stone.

GRACE

I've been walking in dust all day.
The dull ache of memory clogs the mind,
as does the memory of the dull ache.
Trees I once climbed like a panther.
That's a lie   I was never that nimble.
It's hard to know for sure
whether you're in a cage, or flying free.
Right now, I'd like to be eating
at the oyster bar in Grand Central,
or at *Chez Maitre Albert* in Paris.
The wheel keeps turning, the *big*
   to quote Tina Turner   *wheel*,
you know the one I mean.
Mornings in bed I think I'd like
to take you all with me, so nothing
would change except the place.
All those I've loved, all those I left,
all those who left me, all those
who abide.
No man dies, really. It's the world that stops.
Here I am in front of the bathroom mirror
trying to conjugate the future tense
of my favorite French verb: *étonner*.
Je vous étonnerai. I will amaze you.
Cela m'étonne! That astonishes me!
J'ai étonné. I was stunned.
J'étonnais toujours quand je regard sa visage.
I am always surprised when I look at her face.

That's the end of the poem.
I was going to write more,
I thought of what I wanted to say,
or what I was trying to say,
but in the end, I realized
there was nowhere to go after that last line.

When seeing someone's face surprises you,
what else can you say? It's the French, I think.
French has a way of putting a lid on things.
There's something final about it.
Once you say it in French, there's no more to be said.
Mordre les lèvres, to bite the dust.
Ne manquez pas de venir. Don't fail to come.
Elle étais maigre comme un clou. She was thin as a nail.
C'est un livre à lire. It's a book worth reading.
Je bats le pavé. I walk up and down the streets.
Je me suis perdu. I lost myself.
Je perdais la raison. I took leave of my senses.
J'ai perdu mon chemin. I lost my way.
Cette poem est fini. This poem is over. Finished. Done for.

WHAT YOU HAVE TO SURRENDER TO

The page is cold.
I've been bleeding for awhile now.
I came back to see how I was doing, but couldn't face it, and left.
You know, if I find a bottlecap on the sidewalk, I bring it home.

I dreamt once that I was a mermaid.
Another time I dreamt that I was tied to a lampost.
Someone was hitting me with a dark red ribbon.
It was raining and foggy, very mysterious, very scary.

All this suffering belongs to God.
I surrender to a single melody, a single woman, the dark-eyed lady.

The sweetest songs are those that sing of saddest thought blah blah
blah blah, what you have to surrender to if you are going
to love and lay your body at the feet of the lover.

Poor me! Where do I go for flowers in winter?
The swans that skirt the edge of the lake are drunk on kisses.
They confuse sunshine with shade, while speechless dark clouds
drive weathervanes crazy.

If I had the guts, I'd sail without end into the unknown.
But I ain't got the guts. I like it up here in the crow's nest.
You can see land miles before you get there, you can see
the horizon in the distance, always before you, daring you to fall into it.

All the magenta lips that spring up beneath the footsteps of the sun—
it's a haze of blossoms standing in for love, a thousand words of love.
She was in the audience and didn't say a word, afraid I'd gobble her up.
I was on stage, waiting for rescue.

Some days, I do nothing but pay bills and run errands,
tedious details that pull me down
into those small bells of voluptuous insanity,

doing this, taking care of that, constantly moaning
that I haven't written a poem.
My grief, like a birdcage.
Its little door opens, but I dare not fly out.

OBLIVION

Wispy clouds break into white teacups
as I pick up a fresh pencil, one with a point so sharp
it might break with the smallest word, like "of"
or "in" or "at"; I would hardly expect it to survive
a word like Mozambique or disheveled.
When I was in fourth grade, Mrs. Aime yelled at me
during vocabulary tests for the sound effects
I made of explosions and crashes
as I drew pictures of World War I biplanes
alongside the words on the paper
accompanied by smoke and flames,
and the occasional biplane crashing
into the trees below.
I was easily distracted in 4th grade, and today,
I contemplate the landscape outside my window
like a surveyor looking for the best spot to build
a surburban village. I should be paying bills.
But I get distracted by a pencil,
and then distracted by words, and then by a memory
of a moment in the classroom when I had to walk
that tightrope between doing what I was told to do
and doing what my imagination implored.
I haven't the faintest idea how I have managed to survive
this long with no real strategy for living.
I have gone from one distracted impulse to another,
holding onto the only things that have ever mattered to me:
love, fraternity, community.
This is not to say that I have always been kind,
or compassionate. This is not to say that I have never twisted love
for my own purposes, hurt others, taken advantage of affection.
This is not to say that I have not fled from the tribe
and crawled into the hole of my solitude,
where I answer to no one,
not even myself.
Those clouds out there and the hills in the distance

oblivious to the violence we do to ourselves,
even they can't hold my attention for long.
I never grow tired, though, of my desk,
its familiar mess of paper clips and coins,
the letter opener I've had since college,
the Elmer's Glue I haven't touched since Josh was a kid.
The lamps, they're like swans, aren't they,
with their long flexible necks?
And the stacks of books beneath stacks of paper,
and the bills that require me to work,
to go out into the world I love
but could so easily forget if allowed to daydream
too long — where would I be without them?

In a biplane, probably, above the earth.
The poet as Red Baron dropping words
onto the trees below.
Kaboom! and Kaboom! Laying waste to the vocabulary
of my life, from Mozambique to Timbucktoo,
hair disheveled, smoke and flames,
the sweet implosions by which I live.

FORBIDDEN PLANET

Nothing frightens me more than nothing.
Ness.
Angle of vision.
Some of us hoped for war,
a war that would put an end to the other war,
the war that had put an end to the war before it,
and so on.
Can't you make the band stop playing?
It's the same tune over and over again.
My friend the sentence appeared at the front door,
asking to borrow a cup of sugar.
"Figure out what's broken," I said,
"and fix it. If you can't fix it,
break it some more."
I invited the sentence in and now he's still here and refuses to leave.
"Nothingness must be given at the heart of Being."
My high school girlfriend said let's dance the night away
but she forgot her dancing shoes, left them in her mother's coffin,
she's alive today, speaking in tongues.
Later, I found the sentence
under the bed munching an Oreo.

Say something good about God.
If He hears you, he'll be flattered.
If He's digging for worms, he won't.
Writing proves nothing.
Mathematicians, philosophers, social scientists, what do they know
a good band-aid won't fix.
I made him a bowl of soup and he ate it with crackers, the sentence.
Look, sentence, I said, my wife's coming home soon, it's time you go.
Sentence pouted, asked for just one more bowl of soup, stared to cry.
It's midnight now. I'm alone. The house is quiet.
You can hear a pin drop.

BOOK SOUP

You know, I read pages
and pages of books at night
before bedtime
and by the next morning
I find I have to read
the same pages again
and still I'm not sure
what I have read.
Someone is translating someone
else, someone else
is translating herself
and having a tough go of it.
Those untranslatable sentences
keep me from sleeping,
but what keeps me from dying,
I wonder.
You ever fish around in your pocket
in the check-out line
looking for change
to pay for a candy bar
and out comes gum wrappers
and a packet of substitute sugar
you kept handy
and a penny and two nickels
and a key ring but no keys
attached?
Well,

I do that and come up with a handful
of sentences.

> "Art lost its spontaneity in its conflict
> with romanticism."

> "The typical Mystery God of Greek religion is,
> of course, Dionysus."

"A month before monarchical authority
collapsed into bankruptcy, a colossal
hailstorm swept across northern France
and destroyed most of the ripening harvest."

"On a cosmological level, the Big Bang
certainly appears to have a preferred direction."

"In an unplanned economy human beings
unwittingly grant the market control over their lives;
planning the economy is a reassertion
of human sovereignty and an essential step
toward human freedom."

"So on 11 November at 11 a.m., the eleventh hour
of the eleventh day of the eleventh month,
the guns on the Western Front at last fell silent,
leaving both sides to mourn their dead."

The guy at the checkout counter
looks down at the sentences,
then at the candy bar,
and then looks back up at me.
"That's eighty-seven cents," he says.

I reach into my other pocket,
come up with two quarters, a dime,
and this from Rumi, a poem titled "Music":
        "For sixty years I have been forgetful,
        every minute, but not for a second
        has this flowing toward me stopped or slowed."

The boy picks up the sentence by Rumi,
chucks it into the drawer of the cash-register
next to the tens and twenties
and hands me two small sentences in change,
one from a poem by David Igantow:

"I find the dark
close in about me
as I close the book,
and I hurry to open it again
to let its light
shine on my face."

The other, from Descartes' *Meditations*:
    "Since I have been accustomed
    in every other matter
    to distinguish
    between existence and essence,
    I easily believe
    that the existence
    can be separated
    from the essence
    of God,
    and that thus God
    may be conceived
    as not actually
    existing."

I stuff both sentences in my pocket—
the one that held the two quarters,
one dime, and the poem by Rumi—
and walk to my car in the parking lot.

Once back in the car,
I chew on the delicious chocolate candy bar
chuck full of caramel
and peanuts
and head over to Book Soup
to buy another book,
a book full of sentences,
a book full of pages
ready to shine their light
on my face
in the middle of the night.

FIREWOOD

I am old, and have lost something
while retaining my capacity for love.
So many of you out there
I knew forgot remember miss.
Surprise me, won't you?
Open your arms and say welcome.
I will walk into them, still crying.
I will walk into them, unable to breathe,
forgetting the past.
Everytime I thought I knew what love was,
I discovered that love wasn't that at all,
I just thought it was.

It is June, and July will be here,
then August and September, the month of my birth,
and I will fall out of your arms
into the world, again,
back into the rusted earth.
If I am under the ground,
inside this cold earth,
remember I brought love to this planet.
Not much, not enough to make the scale
tilt one way or the other,
but it was enough to put a dent
in your heart,
enough to make trees break
into pieces for firewood,
so when you warm the room in winter,
you can think
the fire came from me,
as it did
when I was alive.

CLOSING THE BOOK

I'm finally able to live in the much sought-after now.
No hard feelings, I hope.
I did my best, limited as my best was
most of the time.
I wanted to leave
you enough firewood
to last through at least one winter.
I know you love fires,
but are afraid of the spiders,
especially the black ones
that nest among the firewood
behind our house,
so I put a stack of wood
in a waterproof box
with an airtight lid,
a kind of coffin made of tupperware.
Remember that day I went to the Container Store?
I was thinking of you squatting at the fireplace,
laying firewood with the architectural precision
of a true fire builder, allowing enough air in
for the fire to breathe.
I want it to last as long as possible
in that drafty room
so you can read
one of those long novels you favor
that create a world you want to live in,
but when you have to close the book
to get ready for your day,
the book is still with you,
you haven't put it down, so to speak.
It lives in you, no effort required,
no need to strain after the feeling—
that's what you said once, anyway:
how moments of comfort
lead to the dread of their loss.
You told me that more than once,

and I, too, believe it's true.
In moments of great happiness,
I hold in reserve some particle of joy,
something I can bank,
when the time comes,
against the embers
of a dying fire.
But I also know
that it's okay to close the book,
it's okay to tear the pages out,
one by one
and cast them onto the embers,
making a blaze out of literature
that will last
throughout the winter.

VOCABULARY WORDS FOR THE DAY

1. FIDGET
2. RUMBLE
3. BOOMING
4. SHRIEK
5. DESTROY
6. VIOLENCE
7. WAXY
8. FUMES
9. SLAIN
10. CONFLICT
11. REVEAL
12. MEADOW
13. REGION
14. NAVIGATOR
15. BRUTAL
16. PEPPERMINT
17. BONUS
18. DEFEAT
19. MASSACRA
20. REVOLT

Jack Gropes
4th Grade
October 12, 1951

BOOM!

BOOM!

KA-BOOM!

KABOOM!!!

KABOOM!!!

KABOOOOM!!!

CRASH!

Made in the USA
San Bernardino, CA
20 November 2013